The Saturn Rocket

by Zoë Clarke

illustrated by Ally Marie

OXFORD
UNIVERSITY PRESS

Nish had ten books on Saturn.
He had a chart showing the planets.

I need a rocket to get there.

5

The shed was a mess.
The boxes were near the back.

Nish cut out some wings.

He cut out a tail.

7

He cut windows in the boxes.
Then he got some red paint.

Nish got in his rocket.
He ran down the garden.

The wings fell off!
The tail fell off!
Nish was sad.

Nish had a hug.

Dad took Nish to the rooftop.

Mum had set up something cool!

Come and see!

Nish took a look at the night.

Saturn is so bright!

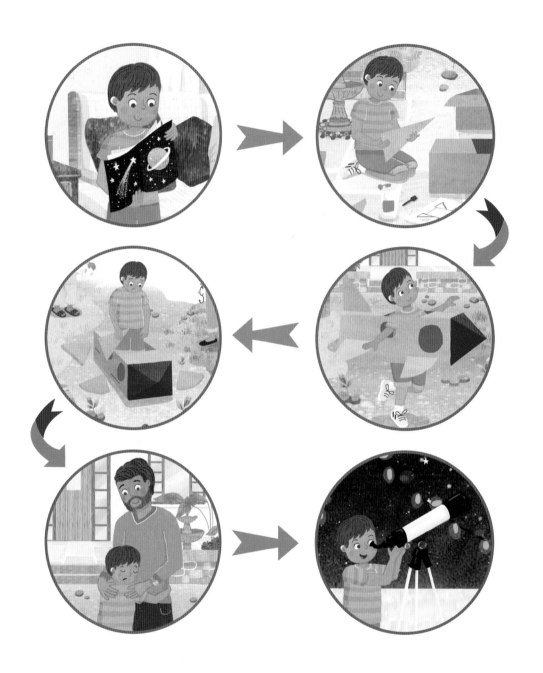

 Encourage the child to use the pictures to retell the story.